ONTARIO

JOSEF HANUS & JOSEF M. HANUS

Personal gift to :

From :

Lake Superior

Canada's largest lake is the world's largest body of fresh water. Lake Superior is the last in the chain of the St. Lawrence-Great Lakes Seaway, and is a favourite spot for summer visitors and outdoor enthusiasts. Numerous beaches and recreational sites are located around this beautiful 82,000 sq km lake.

Neys Provincial Park

Between Terrace Bay and Marathon is situated the beautiful Neys Provincial Park. Its sunny beaches are washed by the waters of Lake Superior. Recreational areas by the lake can be easily reached from Hwy 17.

Aaron Provincial Park

Aaron Provincial Park is located near Dryden, by Hwy 17 and Hwy 72. It is a good spot for bird watching and simple, quiet enjoyment of the area.

Perrault Falls

This photograph of Perrault Falls was taken near Sioux Lookout.

Kenora

An outfitting centre for sportsmen, Kenora is nestled in the northern part of the Lake of the Woods. This mining, pulp and paper town is the closest large community to the Ontario-Manitoba boundary. Famous among sailors is the Lake-of-the-Woods Regatta, when sailboats from around North America sail a one-week course around the lake.

Wawa

Gold fields near Wawa Lake produced gold nuggets worth several million dollars in the short-lived gold rush, from 1897 to 1902. Nestled in the surrounding beautiful scenery, abandoned mines are still accessible just one kilometre from Wawa, now an iron mining town. Next to the tourist centre stands a nine metre statue of a goose. This monument commemorates the opening of the last link in the Lake Superior section of the Trans-Canada Highway on September 17th, 1960.

Kakabeka Falls

Found 22 km west of Thunder Bay, the popular tourist stop of Kakabeka Falls is called the "Niagara of the North." This beautiful 400-hectare Provincial Park has beaches, picnic areas and camping. These falls are 33 metres high.

Arctic Watershed

The Arctic Watershed, elevated at 1660 ft, is located on the Trans-Canada Hwy, just 120 km west of Thunder Bay. From here, all streams flow north into the Arctic Ocean and south into the Atlantic Ocean.

Sioux Narrows

Sioux Narrows Provincial Park, located on the eastern part on the Lake-of-the-Woods, is roamed by such animals as moose, deer, wolves and bears. The park is a preferred spot for camping and fishing. The bridge across Whitefish Bay is the world's longest single-span wooden bridge.

Nestor Falls

The Nestor Falls are located between Kakagi Lake and Lake-of-the-Woods, close to Caliper Lake Provincial Park. The forest here is dominated by red and white pine, cedar and aspen trees.

Lake-of-the-Woods

Known as the 'Thousand Lakes,' the lake connects Ontario and Manitoba with Minnesota. Over 16,000 islands are situated in the waters of the lake. Many of them are occupied in summer months by a multitude of cottagers.

Upsala

The village of Upsala is located by Trans-Canada Hwy 17. The countryside around the village is a spectacular part of North-western Ontario.

Dryden

The pulp and paper town of Dryden is situated on Trans-Canada Hwy 17, near Wabigoon Lake in northwestern Ontario. Highway 17, winding through a stony landscape, is photographed here near Vermillion Bay in Blue Lake Provincial Park, connecting Thunder Bay with Kenora.

Oiumet Canyon

An interesting natural sight located near Dorion, by Black Bay, is the Oiumet Canyon Provincial Park. Cliffs plunge 120 metres to the floor of the 5 km long canyon. The canyon can be reached by Hwy 17, about 65 kilometres east of Thunder Bay.

Greenwich Lake

Photographed in its colourful autumn splendour, Greenwich Lake is nestled in the Cavern Lake Provincial Nature Reserve, near Thunder Bay in northern Ontario.

Rushing River

Flowing through the 160-hectare Rushing River Provincial Park, the river is a popular spot for tourists, photographers and canoeists. Numerous picnic spots, campgrounds, sandy beaches, hiking trails and fishing holes provide attractive activities for summer vacationers.

Thunder Bay

Situated on Lake Superior, this most westerly port on the St. Lawrence Seaway is an important port for Canada's grain industry. Thirty grain elevators fill waiting ships with prairie grain. The city is located on the shores of Lake Superior's lovely Thunder Bay.

Sleeping Giant

Sibley Peninsula is the home of Sleeping Giant Provincial Park. Sheer cliffs soar high above the shore of Lake Superior, and provide a fantastic view of Thunder Bay and Lake Superior. Several viewpoints can be reached via numerous trails. The park's 250 square kilometres occupy most of the Sibley Peninsula, and Sleeping Giant is located at its tip.

Thunder Bay Harbour

Elevators and trains filled with grain from Canada's prairie provinces are a characteristic of Thunder Bay ports. Huge ships begin their long journey through the Great Lakes to the Welland Canal and then through the St. Lawrence River into the Atlantic Ocean, delivering Canadian grain around the world.

Nipigon Bay

Romantic stony beaches create beautiful
environs along Lake Superior, between
Cavers and Nipigon Bay. This photograph was taken from Grant Point.

Helen Lake

Nipigon River courses from Helen Lake
into Nipigon Bay, located in northeastern Ontario. Helen Lake is the halfway
point between Thunder Bay and Sault
Ste. Marie.

Agawa Bay

The lovely beaches of Agawa Bay are a part of Lake Superior. As well as spending summer months on these beaches, Agawa Canyon can be enjoyed in winter months by the 'Snow Train' from Sault Ste. Marie.

St. Joseph Island

St. Joseph Island is located in the channel between Lake Huron and Lake Superior, just 80 km east of Sault Ste. Marie. The beautiful rocky shores are ideal for easy hiking, and swimming is pleasant in its clear, warm waters.

Fort St. Joseph

The National Historic Park of Fort St. Joseph is located on St. Joseph Island. The fort was built in 1796 and was a strategic military post in the War of 1812.

19

Sault Ste. Marie

This is historic downtown Sault Ste. Marie, featuring the city museum.

Ermatinger House

Built in 1814 in the Georgian style, the two-storey Ermatinger House was originally a hotel. This popular historic site of Sault Ste. Marie was later a personal residence, a Court House and a Post Office. Ermatinger House is now a museum.

Sault Ste. Marie Waterfront

Roberta Bondar Park is a picturesque part of the port city of Sault Ste. Marie. The second largest city in steel production (after Hamilton), it is a key link in the St. Lawrence Seaway system, handling over 120 million tonnes of cargo annually.

21

Killarney Provincial Park

Killarney's dramatic scenery and 350 square kilometres of wilderness provide wonderful opportunities for paddling and hiking, making this recreational site—located in Georgian Bay—Ontario's most popular. The entrance to the park is 80 km south of Sudbury, via Hwy 637. Watersports are the favoured activities of outdoor enthusiasts, including long sailing trips on Huron Lake. In the extremely clear water, the lake bottom can be seen as deep as 30 metres.

Spanish River

Spanish River connects Massey and Chutes Provincial Parks with Espanola, a community known as the 'ghost town' in the 1930s Depression.

Massey

Massey is located by the Trans-Canada Hwy, near Espanola and Chutes Provincial Park. The view in this picture is of the Immaculate Conception Paris Church in Massey.

North Channel

The fantastically clear waters of the North Channel, a part of Lake Huron, are located between St. Joseph and Manitoulin Islands. Fresh waters illuminated by the summer morning sun offer a truly natural experience. The North Channel and Lake Huron are attractive to divers, with exploration possibilities among numerous wrecks resting on the lake bottom.

Manitoulin Island

This island, located east of Espanola, between Georgian Bay, Lake Huron and North Channel, is the largest island in the lake. More than 1,550 kilometres of shoreline and numerous beautiful lookouts and sandy beaches are popular with vacationers and sailors. Over 100 lakes offer good fishing for lake trout and northern pike. Native artifacts dating as far back as 12,000 years have been found at several sites on Manitoulin Island.

South Baymouth

The port of South Baymouth is a ferry port, connecting Manitoulin Island with Tobermory on the Bruce Peninsula.

Georgian Bay Islands

This beautiful view of Georgian Bay was taken from Ten Mile Point. Manitowaning Bay and Strawberry Island are just in front of you.

Chantry Island

Chantry Island, the National Migratory Bird Sanctuary, is located in Lake Huron, close to Southampton.

Saugeen Shores

Located on the shore of Lake Huron by the mouth of the Saugeen River, Saugeen Shores include MacGregor Point Provincial Park, Saugeen Indian Reserve and the towns of Sauble Beach, Southampton and Port Elgin. Saugeen Shores are gorgeous sandy beaches on the south part of the Bruce Peninsula. The second photo on this page is of Saugeen River Lighthouse.

The Big Nickel

A 9 metre tall sculpture of a five-cent nickel, originally located in the Canadian Centennial Numismatic Park, was relocated close to Science World in Sudbury. Nickel and copper mined from the Sudbury Basin represent over one third of Ontario's 2 billion dollar annual income from minerals, mined here by two mining companies.

Copper Cliff

The world's tallest smokestack, built on the Copper Cliff, is just six kilometres west of Sudbury. Its 380 metre height allow the smokestack to be seen on Sudbury's skyline from almost anywhere.

Sudbury

A giant meteorite impact is believed to have created the 27 km by 55 km 'Sudbury Basin', millions of years ago. Huge deposits of nickel, copper and other minerals helped to establish the strong and important industrial city of Sudbury on the Northeastern Shore of Georgian Bay. Downtown Sudbury and surrounding areas are pictured here.

29

Kenogami Lake

Kenogami Lake is located near Kirkland Lake in Northeastern Ontario near Trans-Canada Hwy 11. The area became famous in 1912 when gold was found in the Lake Shore Mine claim. Mining equipment from those years can be seen in the Museum of Northern History in Kirkland Lake. Twelve mining companies produced gold in the 1920's. Today, only one company remains. The fall photographs were taken on the place where, 80 years ago, was a thriving area called the 'Lake's Golden Mile.'

Northeastern Fall

Fall is the most colourful time in Ontario. This picture was taken in René Brunelle Provincial Park, near Kapuskasing. Other areas famous for autumn colours are near Wawa, around Peterborough and the Ottawa Valley. Fall in the Thousand Islands and St. Lawrence River area is unforgettable.

Kapuskasing River

The river was photographed in René Brunelle Provincial Park.

Whitefish Falls

A popular area called 'Whitefish Falls' is located on the northern part of Manitoulin Island, close to Charlton Lake and the Bay of Islands.

Little Current

Little Current is well known for its Haweater Festival in August, a horse and riding show. The Hudson's Bay Company was established here in 1856. Numerous wrecks in Lake Huron are a draw for divers in the summer months.

Simcoe Lake – Paradise Point

Over 250,000 lakes have been counted in Ontario! Thousands of them are surrounded by warm beaches, as are those pictured here, photographed close to Orillia on Lake Simcoe. These pictures are of Sandy Beach and Paradise Point, both close to Mara Provincial Park. Residents of Ontario enjoy hot summer days on the beaches. The lakeshores are dotted by thousands of cottages, very popular in Ontario, and local populations are doubled in summer months by vacationers from the cities.

Barrie

A central Ontario community by Lake Simcoe, Barrie is an important industrial and agricultural city. Founded as a supply route in the War of 1812, Barrie is known for its February Winter Carnival, with dogsled races performed on the frozen Kempenfelt Bay, and its annual air show. These photos were taken in the city park, by the lake and in downtown.

Victoria Harbour

A quiet recreational area, Victoria Harbour is situated in Sturgeon Bay, close to Midland and Port McNicoll.

Orillia

The industrial city of Orillia is located by Lake Simcoe in Central Ontario. Winter play on the frozen Lake Couchiching and Lake Simcoe include figure-skating, ice fishing and harness racing. One of the city's interesting sights is the bronze 12-metre high Champlain Monument.

Scugog Shores Museum

The Scugog Shores Museum is located by Port Perry and Port View beach. An attractive display of heritage homes recalls visitors back to the last century. The museum can be reached from Highway 7A.

Balm Beach

Nottawasaga Bay, situated in Southeastern Shore of Georgian Bay, has numerous popular beaches. This photograph was taken on Balm Beach.

Ste. Marie among the Hurons

This extensive and beautifully maintained first European settlement in Ontario was founded by Jesuit priests in 1639. The village 'Sainte Marie among the Hurons' is located by Midland in Midland Bay. This village was restored in the 1960s. Visitors, after an educational movie about life in the 17th century New France, can spend hours among wood and stone houses and see life in the 1600s recreated by costumed guides. To visit the village, one of Ontario's most compelling attractions, is to understand the life of early Christian settlers in Canada and Ontario.

Midland

Located in Midland Bay, the city of Midland has a history connected with the 17th century Huron Nation. The restored village is next to the Huronia Museum. This picture is of the Midland City Library.

Watson's Mill

Watson's Mill is located in Manotick, beside the Rideau Canal in Eastern Ontario.

Brockville

Founded by the Loyalist William Buell in 1784, Brockville is the first loyalist settlement in Canada. The city is located by the St. Lawrence River, just where the area called 'Thousand Islands' begins. The city is named after the 1812 War hero General Isaac Brock. The magnificent Brockville Courthouse, shown here, was built in 1842. Another attraction in the Courthouse Square is the fountain. With its many coloured lights, it is a breathtaking sight in the summer months.

Lagoon City

Private homes are in a park-lake setting in Lagoon City, which is near Sandy Pine beach on Lake Simcoe. Sailboats are moored along gardens. Streets lead across canals, over small bridges. This is a beautiful suburban area in Ontario, and Sandy Beach and Paradise Point are just a few kilometres from here.

Oshawa

The industrial city of Oshawa is located on the shore of Lake Ontario, close to Toronto. Lakeview Park with its sandy beaches is a popular destination. Also shown are Simcoe Street, featuring the United Church, and daycare children playing in the park.

Sunderland

The rye fields near Sunderland.

Victoria Hall

Cobourg, located on the north shore of Lake Ontario, is home to Victoria Hall, built in 1860. Considered the finest municipal building in Ontario, Victoria Hall was opened by King Edward VII.

Queen's University

Queen's University, located on Colborne Street in Kingston, is one of Canada's leading universities. Its first Dean, Thomas Liddell, arrived from Scotland carrying Queen Victoria's Royal Charter. The first picture is of Queen's Theological Hall, in a park by Stuart Street. The library, situated in the university complex was opened in 1994 (second photo).

The Royal Military College

Canada's oldest military academy, The Royal Military College of Canada is located on Point Frederick in Kingston. It was established in 1876 to train officers for Canada's armed forces. In 1878, Her Majesty Queen Victoria granted the College the right to use the Royal prefix 'R.' Since 1789, this area has been utilized as an active military site, and during the War of 1812 it served as the major naval station in Upper Canada.

Fort Henry

The Citadel of Upper Canada, built in 1830 to guard the Rideau Canal, was the largest military establishment in Canada. Situated on Kingston's highest point, the Citadel is the premier historic attraction and outdoor military museum. Over 150 years ago, Fort Henry was Kingston's first line of defence against a war between British Canada and the United States of America. Although the mighty guns of Fort Henry were poised and ready to defend the Citadel, not a single fuse was ignited in a climate of war.

Murney Tower Museum

This imposing structure built in Kingston's port is Murney Tower. Constructed in 1840 as a Martello coastal defense tower, today the tower is a military museum. The tower is situated in Macdonald Waterfront Park.

Port Kingston

Another defense tower was built directly in the waters of Kingston's port.

Kingston

The city of Kingston, once the Capital city of Canada from 1841 to 1843, was first an Indian village. Kingston is located by Lake Ontario, by the mouth of the St. Lawrence River and the Rideau Canal. The city officials started to build the city hall in the expectation that it would become the national legislative building. The second picture is of the St. George Church in Kingston.

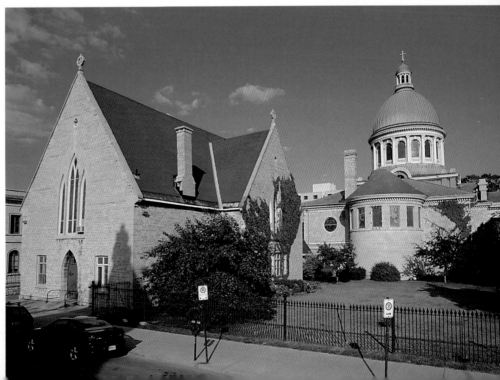

St. Lawrence River

Flowing along the shores of Quebec and Ontario, connecting the Atlantic Ocean with the ports of the Great Lakes, the St. Lawrence River is an inseparable part of the St. Lawrence Seaway. The photographs on this page were taken from Wellesley Island near Brockville.

Hill Island

Located between spans of the Thousand Islands International Bridge, Hill Island is the home of The Thousand Islands Skydeck Tower, which offers a view over 60 km around the area on a clear day, from a viewpoint 120 metres up.

Ivy Lea

A small community close to the International Bridge, Ivy Lea and the area around Parkway is known for the largest stand of Pitch Pine trees in mainland Canada.

Countryside by Wilstead

Thousand Islands Parkway

The 38 kilometre long Thousand Islands Parkway gives a fine view of the St. Lawrence River, with many small islands with private cottages and beautiful ports. The Parkway begins in Butternut Bay and ends by Gananoque, where it joins Macdonald Cartier Freeway.

Georgina Island

St. Lawrence Islands

The Thousand Islands Parkway affords many sport and recreational possibilities on the shores of the St. Lawrence River. Campgrounds, beaches, nature trails and picnic places are popular summer and fall destinations for locals. The Parkway itself offers a pleasing view of countless smaller and larger islands, most owned privately by families or recreational resorts with hotels and docks. Boat owners cruise on the river, observing activity on the small private islands, visiting friends, or just enjoying picturesque vistas of the waterways between the islands.

Rideau Canal

This 200 km canal was built in 1832 after seven years of construction. Connecting Montreal and Lake Ontario via the Ottawa River, the canal bypassed the international waters of the St. Lawrence River, where the transport was not as safe in the early 19th century. After its military purposes were outlived, the canal served small industry as a shipping route for its products. Now, the area around the Rideau Canal is a preferred neighbourhood, popular to tourists and traveled by pleasure craft.

Blockhouse

This is the Blockhouse on the Rideau Canal in Merrickville.

Ottawa – aerial view

The first settler in this area was Nicholas Sparks, who built his farm in 1800, near the place where Sparks Street is today. His homestead was isolated until 1832, when Col. John By and the Royal Engineers completed the Rideau Canal. The area named 'Bytown' began to grow, and its name was changed to 'Ottawa' in 1855. Ottawa was chosen by Queen Victoria to become the capital of Canada in 1857.

Parliament Hill

Parliament Hill rises above the Ottawa River, which is the border with Hull in Quebec. Wellington Street is the site of the Victorian Gothic Parliamentary buildings, built in 1859–1865. The Center Block, with the House of Commons and the Senate, is the most visited site in the city. Thousands of tourists visit the Peace Tower daily to see the city from the highest point of Parliament Hill (87 metres). The East Block houses the Prime Minister's offices and Governor-General's privy councils. The West Block holds offices and committee rooms.

Ottawa River

The Ottawa River, flowing past Parliament Hill, is the natural border between Ottawa, Ontario and Hull, Quebec.

Rideau Canal

Connecting the Ottawa River and Lake Ontario, the 200 kilometres of Rideau Canal begins in Ottawa. It is the oldest city landmark, constructed for military purposes in 1826–1832, when Ottawa was called 'Bytown.' The canal is a chain of lakes, rivers and canal cuts.

Ottawa

The Ottawa region is home to over one million people. Ottawa, the city of history, became the capital of Canada in 1857. This modern city with a European-style downtown is located on the Ottawa River in eastern Ontario.

Madawaska Valley

Autumn yields stunning colours in the Madawaska Valley, where Bancroft is nestled. This area is known for its great variety of minerals, and is attractive for bird watchers and nature photographers. Numerous lakes and streams offer good fishing and excellent hunting. The Bancroft area is a regular summer destination for Toronto residents, who spend weekends and summer vacations in the thousands of cottages, scattered around countless lakes.

Bancroft

From a viewpoint atop a rocky outcrop overlooking the area.

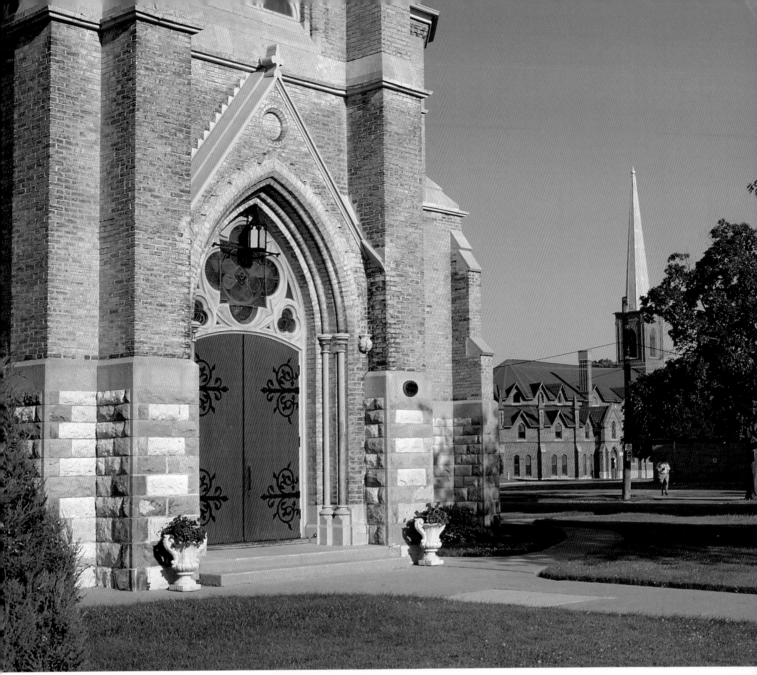

Peterborough

Located 150 km east of Toronto, Peterborough is an attractive place with numerous examples of beautiful architecture, old buildings and churches. The St. George United Church in this picture is one of 58 churches in the area.

Lift Lock

The Peterborough Hydraulic Lift Lock, part of the Trent-Severn Waterway, was opened in 1904. It is the largest hydraulic lock in the world and is Peterborough's most visited landmark.

Niagara-on-the-Lake

Situated on Lake Ontario by the mouth of the Niagara River, the town often called 'the loveliest town in Ontario' is one of the best preserved old towns in North America. The town of Niagara-on-the-Lake was the first capital of Ontario from 1791 to 1796. On this page are the Prince of Wales Hotel and main street.

Niagara River

The Niagara River, 56 km long, is a natural outlet for Lake Erie to Lake Ontario. The elevation difference between the two lakes is 99 metres. Four automobile bridges connect the United States with Canada. Several islands lie in the Niagara River, which is famous for its world class fishing.

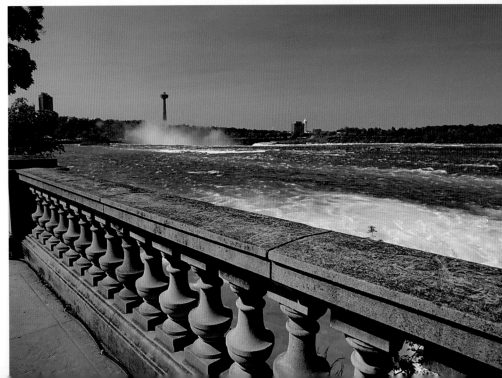

Welland Canal

The Welland canal links Lake Ontario (Port Weller) with Lake Erie (Port Colborne). It is 43 km long, has eight locks with a total lift of 100 metres, and is crossed by 4 railway and 8 automobile bridges. The first Welland Canal was completed in 1829. The second was constructed from 1845 to 1886. The present Welland Canal was built starting in 1913 until its completion in 1932. Thousands of ships use this major part of the St. Lawrence Seaway annually. The above picture was taken by Port Colborne. The large ships need to be precisely maneuvered to within a few centimetres.

Niagara Falls

This most visited attraction in Canada receives over 18 million visitors annually. Niagara Falls is one of the seven wonders of the world and is the largest waterfall in the world, with 3000 cubic metres of water flowing over it each second. More camera film is sold at the falls than anywhere else in the world.

American Falls

Rainbow Bridge is one of 4 highway bridges crossing the Niagara River. Here, the American Falls and the Rainbow Bridge are shown. The American Falls are 330 metres wide.

Niagara Parkway

The most picturesque road in Ontario runs along the Niagara River from Lake Ontario to Lake Erie. The Niagara Parkway was described in 1940 by Sir Winston Churchill as "the prettiest Sunday afternoon drive in the world." The 56-kilometre drive has picnic areas, numerous parks, and trails.

Allanburg Lift Bridge

The lift bridge in Allanburg is one of 8 highway bridges crossing the Welland Canal. Another 4 are railway bridges. Two highway tunnels and one railway tunnel pass under the Welland Canal, a 40 km long bypass of Niagara Falls.

Horseshoe Falls

Three million litres of crystal clear water flow over Niagara Falls every second. The falls occur on the Niagara River some 120 kilometres south of Toronto. The name for Canada's side of the falls, Horseshoe Falls, is given because of their shape. The first person to go over the falls in a barrel was a schoolteacher named Anna Taylor, in 1901. The Horseshoe Falls are 800 metres wide and 50 metres high.

Lake Erie

This lovely view of Lake Erie was taken from Long Point Provincial Park. Lake Erie, 400 km long and 60 km wide, is found in Central Ontario and washes the southern shores of the Niagara Peninsula. Lake Erie connects with Lake Huron by the Detroit River and links with Lake Ontario via the Niagara River. Lake Erie is named for the native peoples who lived on its shores.

Fort Erie

Fort Erie is located in Central Ontario, on the Canada–United States border.

St. Catharines

Wine production is a major interest for many residents of St. Catharines. This city, located in Central Ontario, is a close neighbour to Niagara Falls and Niagara-on-the-Lake.

Waterloo–Kitchener

German immigrants settled here in 1830 and originally named their village 'Berlin.' The twin cities of Waterloo-Kitchener are one of Canada's leading industrial communities. Every year, German residents organize Oktoberfest, a nine-day celebration of German culture.

Highway 401

The busiest Ontario highway begins in Windsor and runs through Niagara Peninsula to Toronto, passing around Lake Ontario and the St. Lawrence River, and on towards the border with Quebec. Highway 401 is 870 km long and is the most important transportation link in Ontario. This picture was taken near London in south Ontario.

Gardiner Expressway

This is the Gardiner Expressway in Toronto.

Ontario countryside

Ontario is the second largest province in Canada, covering 1.6 million square kilometres. This beautiful region covers land from the Arctic tundra to the Great Lakes, bordering Manitoba and Quebec. Thousands of rivers and 250,000 lakes offer world class fishing, and its sunny beaches are full of vacationers all summer long. This lovely ranch and countryside were photographed near Orillia and near the town of Madoc.

London

The comely city of London is the home of the University of Western Ontario. London is a prominent community in the central Niagara Peninsula. Its downtown has three 19th century cathedrals, a university campus with numerous Victorian mansions and a modern gallery, which are fine attractions for the city. Its history began with a native settlement 1,100 years ago.

St. Peter's Cathedral

St Peter's Cathedral is located on Dufferin Avenue in London.

Detroit River

Connecting Lake Huron with Lake St.Clair, the Detroit River is a natural boundary between Windsor, Ontario and Detroit, Michigan. The Detroit river is spanned by the Ambassador Bridge, and a tunnel passes under the river. These photographs are of Riverside Park in Windsor, with the view of the car manufacturing city of Detroit, and of the Ambassador Bridge, which joins to Highway 401.

Ambassador Bridge

The Ambassador Bridge is the world's longest international suspension bridge.

Windsor

Ontario's southernmost city, is located on the western point of the Niagara Peninsula. It is connected to the US by the Ambassador Bridge and a tunnel. Windsor is Canada's busiest point of entry. Over 30 million people cross the river from Detroit yearly. Points of interest in Windsor are the Assumption University, The Art Gallery of Windsor, the Hiram Walker Historical Museum and the International Freedom Festival—a week of concerts, sporting events and parades.

Sarnia

Sarnia, Canada's largest producer of petrochemical products, is located by Lake Huron and the St. Clair River. Besides oil refining, companies in Sarnia produce 12 percent of the world's synthetic rubber. St. Clair River is crossed by the Bluewater International Bridge, connecting Sarnia with Port Huron. In these photographs are the Chemical Valley and the Bluewater International Bridge.

Lake Huron

Lake Huron is the central part of the Canadian Great Lakes. Its blue waters are dotted by hundreds of small islands. The shores of Manitoulin Island, the world's largest fresh water island, are washed by the waters of Lake Huron.

Cove Island

Cove Island is located close to Tobermory and is a part of the Bruce Peninsula National Park.

Toronto

The Capital city of Ontario is home to 3 million people. Toronto's City Hall, located on popular Nathan Phillips Square, was completed in 1964. The ultra-modern architecture of its two curved concrete and glass towers framing the central building is popular with locals who use the plaza as a resting place during the day and as a skating rink in winter.

Wellington Street

This is a historic picture of Wellington St. East and Market Square, taken in 1987.

CN Tower

Toronto's CN Tower is the highest free standing tower in the world. On a clear day, the view, stretching for 150 km around Toronto, is an unforgettable experience. The CN Tower was completed in 1975, and is 553.33 metres tall. In summer, 10,000 people visit the tower daily, using world's highest elevator for the experience of seeing the city from 477 metres up.

Toronto visitors

The fastest growing North American city, Toronto attracts over 15 million visitors yearly.

Toronto Downtown

Toronto is the most expansive city in North America. Its developmental explosion began in the 1960s. The downtown area can best be seen from the CN Tower. The Old City, Wellington Street, Chinatown, Yorkville, Yonge Street and a charming slice of old downtown, including the St. Lawrence Market, attract locals and sightseers day and night.

Eaton Centre

Toronto's biggest shopping centre, located at Yonge and Dundas, is home to hundreds of stores and boutiques including Canada's largest bookstore chain, *Indigo Books, Music & more,* located at the northwest end of the mall.

Toronto – aerial view

The mega city of Toronto is the business centre of Canada. The downtown core, shown here, is the heart of the city which is home to 80 ethnic communities. Toronto has hundreds of theatres, concert halls, libraries, galleries and museums, and is home to the Canadian Opera Company and the Toronto Symphony Orchestra. Toronto has the third largest theatre centre in the English-speaking world. Toronto's Harbour Front and Toronto Island Park are a playground for locals. Its sunny beaches and hundreds of clean parks are occupied in summer months by locals and tourists alike.

Lake Ontario

The Capital city of Ontario, Toronto covers 260 square kilometres, and is situated on the north shore of Lake Ontario. This third largest lake in Canada is a part of the St. Lawrence Seaway.

Toronto Harbour

A popular recreational site for locals is the Toronto Harbour. A ferry links the city with Toronto Island, the home of a recreational world called 'Ontario Place.'